JOHN CENA
Making a Difference Beyond the Wrestling Ring

By Katie Kawa

KidHaven
PUBLISHING

People Who Make a Difference

Published in 2024 by
KidHaven Publishing, an Imprint of Greenhaven Publishing, LLC
2544 Clinton St.
Buffalo, NY 14224

Designer: Deanna Paternostro
Editor: Katie Kawa

Photo credits: Cover, p. 5 Tinseltown/Shutterstock.com; p. 7 Everett Collection Inc/Alamy Stock Photo; p. 9 dpa picture alliance archive/Alamy Stock Photo; p. 11 Allstar Picture Library Ltd/Alamy Stock Photo; p. 13 Sam Aronov/Shutterstock.com; p. 15 DFree/Shutterstock.com; p. 17 lev radin/Shutterstock.com; p. 18 Kathy Hutchins/Shutterstock.com; p. 20 Fred Duval/Shutterstock.com; p. 21 T.Sumaetho/Shutterstock.com.

Library of Congress Cataloging-in-Publication Data

Names: Kawa, Katie, author.
Title: John Cena : making a difference beyond the wrestling ring / Katie Kawa.
Description: Buffalo, New York : KidHaven Publishing, [2024] | Series: People who make a difference | Includes bibliographical references and index.
Identifiers: LCCN 2023010436 | ISBN 9781534544291 (library binding) | ISBN 9781534544284 (paperback) | ISBN 9781534544307 (ebook)
Subjects: LCSH: Cena, John–Juvenile literature. | Wrestlers–United States–Biography–Juvenile literature. | Motion picture actors and actresses–United States–Biography–Juvenile literature. | Philanthropists–United States–Biography–Juvenile literature.
Classification: LCC GV1196.C46 K3 2024 | DDC 796.812092 [B]–dc23/eng/20230306
LC record available at https://lccn.loc.gov/2023010436

Printed in the United States of America

Some of the images in this book illustrate individuals who are models. The depictions do not imply actual situations or events.

CPSIA compliance information: Batch #CSKH24: For further information contact Greenhaven Publishing LLC at 1-844-317-7404.

Please visit our website, www.greenhavenpublishing.com. For a free color catalog of all our high-quality books, call toll free 1-844-317-7404 or fax 1-844-317-7405.

Find us on 📘 📷

CONTENTS

NOT SO SCARY

Professional wrestlers are **tough**. They make a living fighting in front of an audience. Even though professional wrestlers play parts like actors do, some of them might seem scary to meet outside the ring where they fight.

One wrestler who isn't scary beyond the ring is John Cena. In fact, many kids who are sick wish to meet him, and he makes their wishes come true. John has found fame as a wrestler, an actor, and an author, but he believes it's even more important to be known for helping others. He **inspires** people around the world to never give up!

In His Words

"Be who you are regardless of who you are with."

— Tweet from January 2020

John Cena knows that what he does in the wrestling ring is important, but it's what he does beyond it that matters even more. He wants to make a difference by sharing joy with people who need it.

ONE OF THE BOYS

Many kids grow up watching wrestling, including John Felix Anthony Cena. John was born on April 23, 1977, in West Newbury, Massachusetts. He has four brothers, and they would sometimes fight each other, pretending to be like the wrestlers they'd watch on TV. John's dad, who's also named John, worked in the world of wrestling as an announcer.

John liked exercising and lifting weights. At Springfield College in Massachusetts, he studied exercise physiology—the science of how the human body works during and after exercising. After he finished school in 1999, he moved to California to start the next part of his life.

In His Words

"I honestly believed everything I saw … It's something you can lose yourself in."

— Interview with *Men's Journal* magazine from May 2018 about watching wrestling as a kid

John also played football at Springfield College. He grew up to be very strong!

EARLY WRESTLING SUCCESS

When John first moved to California, he had dreams of being a bodybuilder—someone who's known for how big and strong their **muscles** are. He worked at a gym to make money, and while he was working there, he met someone who told him to take wrestling classes.

John took classes and wrestled as part of Ultimate Pro Wrestling (UPW) in 2000. He won the UPW **championship** that same year! John then began wrestling with Ohio Valley Wrestling (OVW) in 2001. OVW trained wrestlers for what's now known as World Wrestling Entertainment (WWE)—the top organization, or group, in professional wrestling.

In His Words

"When called upon, do your best. That's all anyone can ask."

— Tweet from January 2020

When John began wrestling, he used the name "The Prototype" for the character he played in the ring. After a while, he became known by his real name.

A STAR IN THE RING

John's WWE **career** began to take off in 2002, which was when he had his first match on TV as part of a show called *SmackDown*. Two years later, he won his first major WWE championship on his own—the United States Championship.

In 2005, John won his first world championship with WWE. That year, he joined a part of the organization called Raw, which has its own TV show with the same name. John's WWE star continued to rise. As of 2023, he's won 16 WWE world championships, which is tied for the most of all time.

In His Words

"Respect everyone, even your enemies and **competition**."

— Interview with *Men's Fitness* magazine from April 2013

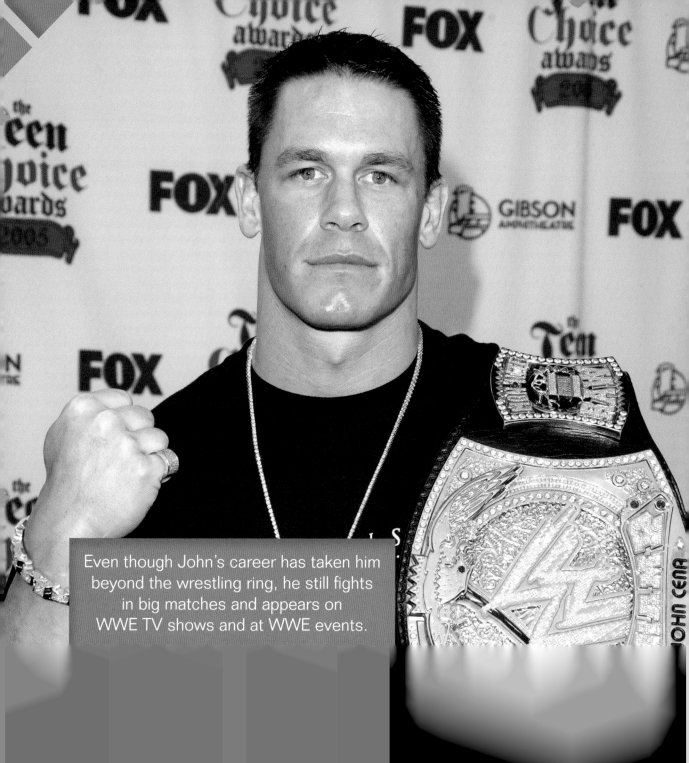

Even though John's career has taken him beyond the wrestling ring, he still fights in big matches and appears on WWE TV shows and at WWE events.

INSPIRING WORDS

As John rose to WWE fame, he became known for certain catchphrases, or things he said often. One of those is "Never Give Up."

John inspires people with his words, especially on **social media**. He often posts positive messages on Twitter about working hard, believing in yourself, and respecting others. In 2021, John collected his most inspiring words for his book *Be a Work in Progress: And Other Things I'd Like to Tell My Younger Self*. That same year, he also came out with a book for kids called *Do Your Best Every Day to Do Your Best Every Day*.

In His Words

"Sometimes you can be so prepared, and still fail … [But] no matter how great the setback, how **severe** the failure, you never give up."

— Speech given at the 2009 WWE Slammy Awards

John has also written a series, or set, of books for children called the *Elbow Grease* books. The first book in the series, called *Elbow Grease*, came out in 2018.

ON THE BIG SCREEN

John has been a familiar face on TV screens for years because of his wrestling career, but he's now become a famous movie star too. In 2006, he starred in the action movie *The Marine*. Other action movies he's been a part of include *F9: The Fast Saga*, which came out in 2021, and *Fast X*, which came out in 2023.

John has also done voice acting in movies for kids, such as *Ferdinand* in 2017 and *Dolittle* in 2020. He's even starred in a superhero TV show called *Peacemaker*, which began in 2022.

In His Words

"If you have any chance of success, you have to really, really prepare as much as you can."

— Interview with *British GQ* magazine from March 2022

John also played Peacemaker in the 2021 movie *The Suicide Squad*. He's shown here dressed up as the character.

15

MAKING WISHES COME TRUE

John has played a hero on TV shows and in movies, but he's also known as a hero to hundreds of kids in real life. For more than 20 years, John has worked with the Make-A-Wish Foundation. This is an organization that grants the wishes of kids who are very sick. Many kids wish to meet someone famous, and John is a popular choice.

In 2002, John granted his first wish. By late 2022, John had granted his 650th wish, which set a world record! John has said he loves having the chance to make sick kids and their families happy.

In His Words

"I can't say enough how cool it is to see the kids so happy, and their families so happy. I truly want to show them that it's their day."

— Video posted on the WWE YouTube channel in October 2015, celebrating his 500th wish granted with Make-A-Wish

John plays a big part in raising awareness about the work Make-A-Wish does too. This means he helps spread the word about how this organization helps people.

17

NO PLACE FOR HATE

John has helped kids in other ways too. He's been a part of different antibullying **campaigns** throughout his career. John was bullied when he was a kid, and he's shared his story to help kids who've been bullied feel less alone and hopeless.

In 2016, John appeared in a video called "We Are America," which celebrates **diversity** across the United States. John believes in taking a stand against hate and supporting others. This is why he gave money in June 2020 to the Black Lives Matter organization. He wanted to help fight **racism** and create positive change.

In His Words

"Every once in a while we need to be reminded everyone is welcome here [in the United States]."

— Interview with *Sports Illustrated* magazine from December 2018

The Life of
John Cena

1977
John Felix Anthony Cena is born on April 23 in West Newbury, Massachusetts.

1999
John finishes school at Springfield College in Massachusetts.

2000
John begins training with UPW and wins the UPW championship.

2001
John joins OVW.

2002
John wrestles in his first *SmackDown* match and grants his first wish for Make-A-Wish.

2004
John wins his first WWE United States Championship.

2005
John wins his first world championship for WWE and joins Raw.

2006
John stars in the movie *The Marine*.

2016
John's "We Are America" video comes out.

2018
John's first *Elbow Grease* book comes out.

2021
John acts in the movies *F9: The Fast Saga* and *The Suicide Squad*, and he comes out with two books—*Be a Work in Progress: And Other Things I'd Like to Tell My Younger Self* and *Do Your Best Every Day to Do Your Best Every Day*.

2022
John begins starring in the TV show *Peacemaker* and grants his 650th wish with Make-A-Wish.

2023
John stars in the movie *Fast X*.

John first found fame in the wrestling ring, but now he's famous for many different things, including helping others.

KINDNESS MAKES A BIG DIFFERENCE

John Cena has been working hard for many years, and he's not showing any signs of slowing down! He has more wrestling events and TV appearances planned, more movies coming out, and more wishes to make come true.

John's life shows what can happen when you work hard and have a positive attitude, or way of thinking. That's a lesson he took beyond the wrestling ring, and it's a lesson he inspires others to take with them too. No act of kindness—from writing a positive post on Twitter to spending time with someone who's sick—is too small to make a difference.

In His Words

"Each day try to become a little less perfect and a little more brave."

— Tweet from July 2018

Be Like John Cena!

If you use social media, use it to spread positive messages.

If you see someone being bullied, help them, and remind them they're not alone.

If you know someone who's sick or hurt, spend time with them to cheer them up.

Talk openly about problems such as racism.

Raise money for the Make-A-Wish Foundation or another group that helps kids who are sick.

Raise money for groups that fight racism, bullying, or other forms of hatred.

Learn more about how important diversity is.

John Cena has big muscles, but they're not what he uses to make a big difference in the world around him. No matter how small or how young you are, you can follow in his footsteps to help others!

GLOSSARY

campaign: A set of activities or events meant to produce a certain result.

career: A period of time spent doing a job or activity.

championship: A contest to find out who's the best player or team in a sport.

competition: A person or group one is trying to beat in a contest or game.

diversity: The quality or state of including many different kinds of people.

inspire: To move someone to do something great.

muscle: A part of the body that produces motion.

racism: The practice of treating others poorly because they are part of a different race, or group of people who look alike in certain ways. This word also relates to governments and societies that allow one race to be treated better than others.

severe: Causing worry or harm.

social media: A collection of websites and applications, or apps, that allow users to interact with each other and create online communities.

tough: Able to deal with hard things and to work very hard.

FOR MORE INFORMATION

WEBSITES

IMDb: John Cena

www.imdb.com/name/nm1078479/

The Internet Movie Database is the place to go for facts about John Cena's career and the movies and TV shows he's been a part of.

WWE Community

community.wwe.com

This website provides links and stories about ways WWE wrestlers, including John Cena, are helping people in their community.

BOOKS

Cena, John. *Do Your Best Every Day to Do Your Best Every Day*. New York, NY: Random House, 2021.

Fishman, Jon M. *Pro-Wrestling Superstar John Cena*. Minneapolis, MN: Lerner Publications, 2019.

Gagne, Tammy. *John Cena*. Minnetonka, MN: Kaleidoscope Publishing, 2020.

INDEX